HOW TO HUNT

FOR KIDS 6-12

25+

SURVIVAL ACTIVITIES FOR A SAFE HUNTING TRIP. LEARN TO BUILD A FIRE, USE FIRST-AID AND PUT UP A SHELTER IN THE WOODS.

BY

JOEY ARMSTRONG

Disclaimer Notice

This book is written and published independently. Please keep in mind that the material in this publication is solely for educational and entertaining purposes. All efforts have provided authentic, up-to-date, trustworthy, and comprehensive information. There are no express or implied assurances. The purpose of this book's material is to assist readers in having a better understanding of the subject matter. The activities, information, and exercises are provided solely for self-help information. This book is not intended to replace expert psychologists, legal, financial, or other guidance. If you require counseling, please get in touch with a qualified professional.

By reading this text, the reader accepts that the author will not be held liable for any damages, indirectly or directly, experienced due to the use of the information included herein, particularly, but not limited to, omissions, errors, or inaccuracies. You are accountable for your decisions, actions, and consequences as a reader.

About the Author

Author, lecturer, and outdoor enthusiast Joey Armstrong takes great pleasure in encouraging children to read, write, and enjoy the outdoors. In his several books on Hunting Experiences, young readers accompany him on incredible hunting and fishing expeditions. Joey Armstrong, a renowned speaker, uses his unique outdoor theme to motivate, instruct, and enthrall children. One of his favorite activities is going to school and talking to youngsters.

TABLE OF CONTENTS

FEW WORDS FOR PARENTS

Dear Parents,

The world is advancing at a fast pace. Technology is changing everything, at a speed unimaginable. There is no doubt this evolution has made our lives better in every aspect. We are much wealthier, healthier, and happier today than we ever were in the past.

The outdoors industry has grown astronomically, especially over the past few years. While the pandemic was brutal and devastating for almost all of us, it did act like a corrective measure when it comes to passion for the outdoors. It pushed us off our couches and into the wilderness. All of a sudden, the world realized it was gradually disconnecting itself from the great outdoors and becoming more and more absorbed by technology. It pressed the reset button and we started seeing growing trends for outdoors activities across the globe. State and National Parks have more visitors now than ever before.

As the trend grows, the awareness and knowledge for acquiring proper survival skills and techniques must also grow. Learning survival skills can be intimidating, but you'd be amazed at how much you can grasp by just trying. We are most adaptable to new skills and techniques if we start at an early age. Our bodies and brains grow rapidly and act like sponges. They are receptive and willing to absorb as much information as we throw at them in those youthful years. They are also resilient and quick to adjust and therefore teaching survival skills at an early age is ideal. And thanks to technology, the advancement in tools and gadgets available today is mind blowing. Not only these gadgets have become astoundingly more capable and efficient, they are much more affordable and accessible.

We are running out of excuses not to regularly engage in outdoor activities. The benefits are limitless and with proper guidance, we can teach our youth to make the most out of their trips. After carefully going through this guide, you can be much better prepared for an outdoors adventure in the woods with family and friends. These activities will help you teach your young ones to be more responsible, self-sufficient and confident for their next hunting expedition. Most importantly, it will boost their self-belief and promote a positive outlook towards everything else in life. Again, parental guidance is mandatory.

Children should learn survival skills to understand how to navigate through nature because it gives them a sense of security and independence when they are out in nature and hunting. Learning how to maneuver through a forest can have several additional lessons, such as being around nature frequently presents challenges and develops intuitive problem-solving skills, which helps them gain confidence in their capacity to deal with unforeseen circumstances. Survival skills not only help children traverse the wilderness but also boost self-belief and promote faith in their abilities.

INTRODUCTION

Children, who learn about survival in the wilderness, foster confidence, improve self-esteem, offer required exercise, and forge a connection with nature.

Hunting is an excellent method for kids to spend time outside and disconnect from technology. With this exercise, a youngster can have the best outdoor adventure and learn to truly appreciate the outdoors and the natural world around them. Spending time outside has various health advantages, including exercising in the open air. Hunting is believed to lower stress, which promotes your child's physical and mental development.

Could your kid survive if they were lost in the wild? Would they be able to keep themselves safe until they receive required aid?

As a bush-craft practitioner and instructor, I devote much of my time to teaching people about survival in the outdoors, sustainable practices, and resource management. More significantly, I'm a father, passionate about passing on those talents and igniting the outdoor curiosity in the next generation.

I not only talk about camping and survival when I ask to get the kids outdoors. Survival skills improve mental health, well- being, confidence, and they also help youngsters to appreciate nature and environment. They also improve safety, resilience, and capability in emergencies. My children, aged 8, 6, and 2, all understand the recovery position and how to dial the helpline in a medical emergency. If my mother or I am hurt or become disabled at home or while we are out and about, they have all information about how to put us in the recovery position. Having this information gives me peace of mind that they won't just be able to help us in an emergency but also if a friend, classmate, or neighbor gets wounded.

Although, you are not preparing your children to be Mad Max-style survivor machines capable of battling zombies, you're merely demonstrating the benefits of outdoors and the enjoyable talents they might learn.

Ensuring everyone in your family has the necessary survival skills is essential to survive successfully. They're also useful for camping and emergencies. Kids are included in this. It's important to teach children age-appropriate basic survival skills to set them up for success in life. While young children won't be much assistance in an emergency, you can start preparing your child for one as early as four or five.

Everyone who spends much time in nature knows that things can change quickly. An animal may attack, a storm may blow in, someone may get hurt, or a bug may sting. A hike that seemed safe at first might rapidly turn disastrous. None of this is being said to terrify you or make you avoid being outside. But as we teach our children to enjoy being outside, we also need to provide them with the skills necessary to handle any emergencies that may arise.

Children should be prepared for the unexpected throughout their lives by keeping a level head, having an emergency kit, and learning some basic wilderness survival skills. Meanwhile, learning bush-craft techniques is a lot of fun. They are helpful in a survival crisis, no doubt. Yet you and your teen can also enjoy them as a fun challenge!

Kids can learn fundamental survival skills and how to utilize the environment around them by going camping. Packing a bag with necessary items, such as a map, compass, flashlight, fire starter, first aid kit, rope for knot tying, food to cook, etc., and practicing how to utilize them in the outdoors can be an exercise in readiness training. Also, you can arrange educational activities like a guided fishing excursion or a hunting expedition for older children. Along with learning the fundamentals of survival, children will also learn how to rely on themselves rather than the contemporary conveniences and technology they are used to. They can apply these talents to solve problems in various other spheres of their lives.

Unfortunately, hunting is a disappearing sport, but you may still take action. By taking a child hunting, you can help preserve the sport and foster their development into an accomplished hunter. Through hunting, children learn how to aim; shoot, and field dress an animal. Also, it inspires a lifetime desire to grow one's own food, spend time outdoors, and protect the environment. It's one of the best pastimes to encourage in a child since it fosters courage, tenacity, and resilience, unlike other activities they frequently partake in. It also gives the little ones a chance to feel special when they're out in the woods hunting for a game, just like mom and dad.

This book includes various engaging and informative activities that teach them about hunting and survival safely and responsibly. Here are some ideas of what the book contains:

Basic hunting safety: Teaching kids the basics of hunting safety, such as how to handle firearms and other hunting equipment, how to identify and avoid hazards in the environment, and how to communicate with hunting partners.

Hunting gear and equipment: Explaining the different types of hunting gear and equipment, including firearms, archery equipment, camouflage clothing, and other gear that hunters might use.

Wildlife identification: Teaching kids how to identify different types of wildlife, including game animals, birds, and other animals they might encounter while hunting.

Hunting techniques and strategies: Explaining different hunting techniques and strategies, such as stalking, still hunting, and calling. Providing examples of how to use each technique effectively.

Survival skills: Teaching kids important survival skills, such as how to build a fire, how to find and purify water, how to build a shelter, and how to navigate in the wilderness.

First aid and emergency skills: Teaching kids basic first aid and emergency skills, such as how to treat cuts and bruises, how to respond to a snake bite or other injury, and how to signal for help in case of an emergency.

Outdoor ethics: Teaching kids about respecting the environment and wildlife and minimizing their impact on the environment while hunting and camping.

Activities and games: Inclusion of fun and engaging activities and games that reinforce the lessons taught in the book, such as scavenger hunts, word searches, and outdoor puzzles.

By including these topics in a kid's hunting and survival skills activity book, children can learn about hunting, survival safely and responsibly while having fun and engaging in hands-on learning.

Before teaching your kids about hunting, start with K-W-L Chart and help your kid.

What I know

What I Want to Know

What I Learned

CHAPTER 1

LOVE FOR THE GREAT OUTDOORS

Do you hunt? Do you intend to foster a passion for hunting in your children? Even though it's not for everyone, hunting can be a great way to spend time with your kids outside. Hunting teaches children perseverance, ethics, responsibility, self-reliance, patience, and respect. It also helps children comprehend the role of conservation of environment, and food chain.

Hunting involves sitting in a duck blind and seeing stunning sunrises or enjoying the deer grazing on the winter wheat. It also involves sitting in a tree stand and taking in the sounds of nature as they reverberate through the forest. A cool October morning when hunting is a time of awareness and tranquility is when people are engrossed in nature and surrounded by serene beauty.

Hence, when kids first show interest in learning to hunt, there is no way to stop them from going on hunting trips with their parents. The much-anticipated fall hunting season starts, as the weather turns cooler. It's the time of year for crisp mornings, crunching leaves, preparing, and finally bringing in that big buck, along with perhaps a few little ones.

This fall, do you have any plans to take your family hunting? There will be a certain amount of magic to that event and many instructive moments; it is important to start preparing them immediately. But how exactly do you do that? And how would you even know whether your kids want to hunt? Your kids will begin learning before you take them on their first hunting trip.

1.1 Reasons to Go for A Hunting Trip

One of the many reasons to take a child hunting is to preserve the culture of conservation for the sake of the future of outdoor recreation. It's no secret that hunters make up the world's greatest conservationist population. The tax money from the sale of guns and ammo goes toward animal conservation. You can take your son or daughter on a hunting expedition. You can also take the neighborhood kids. Even one new, youthful hunter joining your team is a positive move. Of course, increasing the number of young hunters isn't just for conservation. We know the advantages of being in the woods for our bodies and minds. Children need time away from electronics, and spending the day outside is the best remedy.

Many people can be frightened by the thought of hunting with children. However, a fear of hunting often results from ignorance of the activity or a lack of trust in one's abilities to engage in this practice. But you can prevent this by training your children to hunt while they are still very small. Teaching your kids to hunt is a smart idea for various reasons, including the fact that it helps them deal with fear. Some other benefits of hunting are:

- **Youngsters Learn to Pay Attention Through Hunting**

Effective hunting requires a lot of awareness of your surroundings. You must have an eye for small things like animal footprints and the wind's direction. This can teach children the important lesson that they must be keenly aware of their surroundings; a lesson that is becoming more difficult to instill as they have access to more advanced technology.

- **Hunting Brings Kids Outdoors and Fosters Family Bonding**

Effective hunting requires a lot of awareness of your surroundings. You must have an eye for small things like animal footprints and the wind's direction. This can teach children the important lesson that they must be keenly aware of their surroundings; a lesson that is becoming more difficult to instill as they have access to more advanced technology.

- **Hunting Boosts Self-Confidence**

Parents have occasionally witnessed their child's "I can do it alone" attitude. Children aspire to be independent, and it is your responsibility as a parent to raise them to the point where such independence is realistic. Kids' confidence and excitement when doing something for the first time is motivating. Hunting requires a lot of ability. Your kids will feel better about them and be more motivated to learn as they gain and maintain those skills. Also, you will see that as they become older and can complete more tasks independently, their confidence in those abilities, in general, will increase significantly.

- ## Hunting Instills Responsibility

Hunting can be a lot of fun but it also carries much responsibility. Hunters must learn how to use their weapons securely and correctly and kill their prey with a precise, quick shot. Also, hunters must be aware and adhere to the rules and regulations established for the activity. All of this suggests that hunters should be extremely accountable for their actions. It is not a characteristic that will simply apply to hunting; most hunters apply this discipline to other facets of their lives, increasing their overall accountability.

- ## Hunting Improves Physical Well-being

Finding the ideal location by hiking through the woods, moving through dense foliage, or carrying your most recent catch can all be extremely strenuous. You don't have to be a bodybuilder to perform it, but you do need to be in generally good health. Another reason for teaching your kids to hunt is to keep them active. It can be simple to lead a very sedentary lifestyle with all the screen time we talked about previously. Hunting expeditions will not only get your child off the sofa, but they will also introduce them to a way of life or, at the very least, a hobby that will motivate them to maintain their health. This is just another lesson kids can apply throughout their lives.

- ## Youngsters Learn Conservation Through Hunting

Budding hunters must be recognized for their role in conserving the habitat where they hunt. Many hunters instinctively care about the environment and the survival of species. They have a strong connection to land and are genuinely interested in seeing it thrive. By encouraging preservation and rewarding best practices, we ensure a healthy mindset in our youth, and it is essential for a safe future of these lands and helps in its survival and further expansion.

- ## Hunting Educates Children to Value Hard Work

Hunting can instill the value of a hard day's effort in your kids. It's not as simple as stepping outdoors and immediately getting the perfect shot. There is a huge reward for the correct amount of dedication, but a lot of waiting and preparation is required. Children learn from this that they can accomplish their goals if they put up the necessary time and effort. Hunting can be a fun activity and a terrific family learning experience, from principles it teaches the way of life.

- **Learning How to Make Decisions**

Each hunting trip begins with uncasing a bow or firearm and ends with dozens of decisions. Also, every choice has results or repercussions. In extreme circumstances, the results of a poor choice could cause serious harm or even death. Consider entering a dangerous place with a rifle in your hand or climbing into a tree without a safety belt. Moving at the wrong time, startling an animal, or choosing a hunting stand with the wrong wind direction are two other poor choices with less serious consequences. This is why hunting is a terrific way to help kids learn how to make decisions and how those decisions translate to other aspects of life when there are many potential outcomes, like operating a vehicle or choosing a career. Along with the decision-making, it's essential to teach kids the value of being aware of their surroundings and avoiding subject-specific limited vision. For instance, if they aim at an animal, they must know what is beyond it. They must be looking for cars that might run a red light if they are crossing the street at a crosswalk.

1.2 How to Start a Hunting Expedition?

A child should gradually be introduced to hunting. It should be done wisely and in ideal conditions. This lessens the possibility that they may connect the sport with discomfort or boredom. Mother Nature, however, frequently has a way of abruptly changing directions. A good afternoon spent in the stand could rapidly turn bad. With Banks blinds, the effects of the weather can be eliminated. They are sealed to keep out cold air. On those chilly days, an indoor heater can keep you cozy. The inside walls are covered with noise-canceling liners, allowing children to explore and inquire. Bring them a good book and a hearty lunch. That much freedom makes hunting seem more like a fun hobby than a chore.

- **Prepare Kids Mentally**

Mental preparation is essential in helping a child understand and enjoy a new hunting experience. There needs to be a lot of planning done beforehand. You can't just take a child from playing in the backyard and expect them to sit quietly in a blind or see an animal get shot. Let's go through two crucial preparation steps to help you decide when and how to introduce kids to the activity.

When Is the Right Age to Go Hunting?

Depending on where you reside, different age restrictions exist on when a child or young person can possess a firearm and take a big-game animal. States with no upper age limit exist. Additional criteria may relate to hunting as an apprentice or with a mentor and range in age from 10 to 16. A hunter safety course is also required in many states. Find out if your state has a minimum age limit for hunting. The ideal moment to take your youngster on their first hunt is a personal choice. Yet, the hunting custom has become ingrained in many families' cultures without having a clear beginning. It is passed down from one generation to the next and is a component of daily life. Hence, if your child isn't carrying or shooting, they can enjoy the entire hunting experience at any age! To develop your traditions, consider exposing kids to these hunting-related activities. They're an excellent way to impart important field education to children, teach them about safety, and assist in fostering a love of the great outdoors.

How to Describe Hunting to a Child?

There is much more to hunting than simply taking a shot at an animal. It involves discovery, strengthening relationships with loved ones and friends, appreciating nature, wonders of the mountains, woodlands, and wildlife. With kids and even toddlers, it's a good idea to express your excitement and to explain the circle of life, which is nature's way of taking and giving; when something dies, it offers new life to something else. Children should also be informed about what happens during a hunt. Educate them about actual instances. Describe the procedure of taking wildlife and your motivations for hunting, such as food, adventure, conservation, or trophies. Explain in detail the possibility of shooting and killing an animal. Be specific about how you plan to use the meat. Watch their responses. Respond to their inquiries.

- **Engage in Hunting-Related Activities**

Make hunting a regular part of your child's life, not simply something that occurs once a year. Build a strong tradition of family time and respect for the outdoors as hunting related activities offer enjoyment, educational opportunities, and excellent bonding time. Here are some hunt-related activities you can do with kids all year long:

Go out exploring. This is a fantastic chance to give kids a close-up look at animals in the wild. Activities could include seeing animals and hunting for food sources.

Share trail cam images. Children love animals! Show them the cool pictures and videos you captured with your trail camera.

Plant food plots. Nothing beats getting in a tractor with your kid, taking care of land, and chatting about deer.

Recreate hunting circumstances. Children can see animals up close and learn what an actual hunt might be like by spending time in a blind or canvassing your land.

Assist harvest animals. Teach children that taking care of an animal means using it for food. Show kids how to cook the meat they've collected and how to eat it.

- ## Hunt with Integrity

It is essential to recognize that the individual who spends most of the time with a child has the greatest influence on developing good hunting practices. Therefore, it is crucial to cultivate a strong moral character and a deep respect for the land, animals, people, and weapons before guiding young people in these pursuits. Additionally, participating in excellent youth programs can prepare and educate children on responsible hunting practices. Remember to exercise caution when guiding children and always prioritize safety and ethical conduct.

1.3 Plan Ahead: What to Do?

Children must be taught to hunt properly if you don't want to permanently turn them off during the activity. Therefore, you need a plan. When hunting with friends, you may risk it, but you cannot take a 10-year-old on a hunting trip without planning ahead.
These are some things to think about.

- ## Gear that Works

You must choose a hunter outfit of your child if you want them to behave like one. Your little gunner will feel more at home and be protected from the weather if they are dressed appropriately and have the necessary gear. Below are the essential items they will require.

Clothing

Your child needs orange or red color jackets and camouflage when it comes to hunting attire. Wearing blazing orange helps ensure safe hunting because while your other hunters can spot your presence but deer cannot distinguish red or orange color. Make sure that they are dressed comfortably while also keeping them warm and dry. If you live in the north, snow pants might seem like a smart idea, but once you're 100 yards into the woods and the swish is louder than a rocket, you'll know they're not. Children also require a raincoat, hat, gloves, scarf, thick socks, boots, and long underwear.

Equipment

Even if the main equipment is a rifle or a bow for hunting, you'll need a few more things. Carry hand warmers, a kind of seat cushion, a vest or backpack to store ammunition and food also a gun, of course. Depending on what you're hunting, your child should use a different type of gun, but it should be small enough in size and length for them to manage easily.

- **Know where you're going:**

If you are scouting or going on hunting, go for an active but not overly congested place. Ensure that it is accessible and not too far away.

No child has high patience, especially if there isn't ample action. Plan to walk around every hour to keep your child interested in the hunt rather than making him bored.

- **Think about using a blind:**

A hunting blind is a structure that hides the hunter so that the prey can finally come into full view and within shooting distance. Hunting blinds come in various shapes and sizes; some are moveable, while others are permanent. Plan how you will be going to use that blind. Inform and guide your kids about its safety and how to use it. Play

Hunters often use hunting blinds to conceal themselves from prey and increase their chances of a successful hunt. While waiting for the game animal to come into view, hunters can engage in a variety of games to pass the time and keep themselves entertained. Here are some games that can be played in a hunting blind:

- **Spotting game** - This game involves trying to spot different animals in the surrounding area. Players can keep track of the number and type of animals they see, and the person who spots the most wins.
- **Charades** - Players can take turns acting out different animals, plants or hunting scenarios while the others try to guess what they are.
- **Trivia** - Players can test each other's knowledge of hunting, wildlife, or local flora and fauna with trivia questions.

- **Card games** - Compact card games like poker, rummy, or go fish can be played in the blind to pass the time.
- **Storytelling** - One person starts telling a story, and each person in the blind adds a sentence or two until the story is complete.

Remember, safety should always be the top priority when playing games in a hunting blind. Avoid loud or sudden movements, and make sure that all firearms are unloaded and stored safely.

Using a blind game with kids the night before going hunting with them can be a helpful way to prepare them for the experience while also emphasizing the importance of safety and responsible hunting practices. Here are some potential benefits:

Familiarity with the environment: The blind games can help children become more familiar with the hunting environment and the types of animals they may encounter. This can help them feel more comfortable and prepared for the hunt.

Safety preparation: The blind games can also be used to reinforce important safety measures, such as staying quiet and still and not moving or disturbing the natural environment. This can help children understand the importance of responsible hunting practices and reduce the risk of accidents or injuries.

Learning opportunity: The blind games can be a fun and engaging way to teach children about different animal sounds, behaviors, and habitats. This can help them develop a deeper understanding and appreciation of the natural world.

Bonding experience: Participating in blind games with children can be a bonding experience, as it allows shared excitement and anticipation for the upcoming hunt. However, it is important to ensure that the blind games are age-appropriate and do not create unnecessary stress or anxiety for the children. It is also crucial to emphasize that hunting is not a game and requires a responsible and ethical approach. Organize everything a night before and have your youngster lay out their clothes, boots, ammunition, and gun as you pack their luggage.

Remember to pack snacks:

Children grow hungry and thirsty more quickly than adults, and if they are not fed well, it will result in whining. Bring many tasty snacks, as they can serve as a diversion when the woods grow monotonous. Even if you want your toddler to concentrate on the woods, his attention span isn't as lengthy as yours. So bring distractions. Allowing him to bring a calm diversion like a book, coloring supplies, or action figures will prevent you from getting angry.

- ### Know when to give up:

Most kids fewer than 14 won't have the stamina or patience to hunt all day. Plan on staying for three to four hours or less if it's cold. Don't be scared to end a project early if you need to.

- ### Advancement at their rate, not yours:

Don't push your child too hard; let them determine when they are ready. Your child may either be comfortable and excited or not fully ready for it. But once in the woods, things might not be, as they seem. If they're not prepared, it's okay; just demonstrate for them how to do it.

Whether you bag a deer or not, have fun and celebrate a wonderful day in the woods with your friends and kids.

1.4 Safe Hunting

When you go hunting with a young child, you must teach them how to be safe and keep others protected. While hunting safety is frequently neglected, the person you're hunting with is usually unsafe in the woods (38 percent of shooting accidents happen within 16 feet).

You should teach your child three crucial areas of hunting safety and how to handle a gun safely.

Observe your surroundings. Children are prone to distraction, so teach your youngster to remain vigilant while hunting. They ought to be aware of nearby streams, blind spots, and the direction of the route.

Keep an eye out for other hunters at all times. Ensure that your youngster knows that when he goes for hunting, he should always be on the lookout for other hunters, deer or turkey. Anyone can show carelessness and might walk right through your shooting area.

Never shoot unless you are sure. No matter what, instill in your youngster the idea that you should never fire a gun unless you are very sure of the target. You must be certain without a shadow of a doubt that it is neither a deer nor a squirrel. Help him through the shot when it comes to actually firing the trigger. Come near, maintain a steady voice, and remain at ease. Be positive and comforting, taking him from raising the weapon to pulling the trigger step by step.

1.5 Hunting Techniques and Strategies

Teaching hunting techniques and strategies to kids requires careful attention to safety, ethics, and respect for wildlife. Here are some hunting techniques and strategies that can be taught to kids:

Stalking: Stalking involves moving quietly and slowly through the woods to sneak up on game animals. Teach kids how to move quietly, use cover and concealment, and also avoid making noise or movement that could alert animals to their presence.

Still hunting: Still hunting involves finding a good spot to wait and watch for game animals to come into range. Teach kids how to find a good spot, stay quiet and still, and also remain patient and alert.

Calling: Calling involves using a device to mimic the sounds of an animal, such as a deer or turkey, to attract it into range. Teach kids how to use a call, identify the sounds of different animals, and use cover and concealment to remain hidden while calling.

Tracking: Tracking involves following the signs left by animals, such as tracks, droppings, and other clues, to locate them. Teach kids how to identify different animal tracks, read other signs left by animals, and follow tracks quietly and carefully.

Archery: Archery involves using a bow and arrow to hunt game animals. Teach kids how to use a bow safely and accurately, select appropriate arrows and broad heads, and aim and shoot at game animals.

Showing kids, the importance of safety, ethics, and respect for wildlife while hunting is important. Teach them to follow all hunting laws and regulations. Teach them to only take shots they are confident they can make accurately. Teach them to always treat animals humanely. By learning these hunting techniques and strategies responsibly and respectfully, kids can develop important skills and a sense of responsibility for the environment.

• Hunting Procedure

Hey, little adventurer! Are you ready to learn about the exciting world of hunting? Hunting is a fun, and fascinating activity humans have enjoyed for thousands of years. Today, we will discuss the basic hunting procedure and how it works.

First, you need to pick the right gear. You'll need a hunting rifle or bow and arrow, appropriate clothing and boots, and a backpack to carry your supplies. You may also need a hunting permit and tags, depending on the type of animal you're hunting and where you're hunting.

Next, it's time to find your prey. You'll need to look for signs of animals in the area, such as tracks, droppings, and bedding areas. You can also use binoculars or a spotting scope to help you spot animals from a distance.

Once you've located your prey, it's time to get into position. You'll need to move slowly and quietly to avoid alerting the animal to your presence. You'll want to position yourself where you have a clear shot at the animal and where you can safely take your shot.

You'll want to aim carefully and ensure you're within range when taking your shot. Depending on the animal you're hunting, you may need to take a shot from a distance, or you may need to get closer to ensure a clean, ethical kill.

After you've taken your shot, following up quickly and carefully is important. You'll want to track the animal's movements and ensure it's down for good. Then, you can approach the animal and begin the process of field dressing and processing the meat.

Hunting is an exciting and challenging activity that requires skill, patience, and respect for the animals we hunt. It's important to always follow safety guidelines and hunting regulations and treat the animals and the environment with care and respect.

1.6 Mistakes to Be Avoided

The wrong introduction to hunting can make children never want to go again.

Kids should enjoy going hunting with you. Achievements are lovely but try not to set unrealistic expectations.

Got it, let me explain this with my real-time story.

I looked forward to taking my two young boys on their first turkey hunt. I imagined a peaceful morning in the blind while waiting for the birds to arrive. I already had a long conversation with my kids and had clarified what a luxury going hunting would be. I was confident they would act in a way that could demonstrate their appreciation for the chance. Of course, I showed patience and expertise as I imparted my hunting knowledge and our cherished family hunting traditions but didn't guide them really well about the adventure ahead.

The next morning, our much-anticipated first turkey hunt was ruined by screaming fights, meltdowns, and even a few tears before we reached the blind.

In all seriousness, I was at fault for our unpleasant encounter.

I now see that I made a lot of errors. Although parents usually mean well when they take their kids hunting, a few missteps can stop kids from falling in love with hunting. Here are some mistakes that commonly parents do while hunting with kids:

- **Unfounded Expectations**

It was my very first error. Little children will be agitated and boisterous. They'll be curious and want to learn more. Thus, you should anticipate and motivate them to do so. Keep hunts brief and energetic to avoid keeping your kids sitting for extended periods. Small game hunts are excellent choices since they allow you to converse and move about. If you take a young child deer hunting, keep the hunt brief—no more than 45 minutes or an hour—and keep moving. Go slowly through the forest. Discuss what you've seen and heard by pausing. It's all about having a good time.

- **Lack of Emphasis on Safety**

When hunting with children, safety should always come first. Anyone can have an accident, but the likelihood is increased while hunting with a novice. Refrain from assuming that your child is knowledgeable about safe hunting practices. Spend some time educating them about safety and serving as a role model for safe conduct and habits.

- **Prioritizing Other Objectives Above Fun**

Little children won't want to go hunting again if they don't enjoy it the first few times. To promote learning and participation, turn identifying birds or trees into a game and gather leaves, rocks, and other objects. Let children bring along some amusement for when the action calms down, such as books, crayons and toys.

- **Not Being Well Prepared**

A hunt will turn ugly if you take youngsters hunting with poor food, drink, or equipment supplies. Children experience hunger and thirst more frequently than adults and a grumbling stomach makes a child cranky. Bring plenty of food and beverages to break up the monotony. Bring extra warm clothes and rain gear for the kids because they get cold faster than adults. Moreover, keep Band-Aids, antibiotic creams, and other first-aid supplies on hand in case your child suffers a minor injury. If you're a parent of young children, you know Band-Aids' power.

- ## Children Being Expected to Shoot Before They're Ready

Although there is no defined age at which a youngster can shoot their first animal, it is up to you to decide when the child is ready. Allowing a child to use a firearm or kill an animal before they are ready emotionally or physically may snuff out their enthusiasm for hunting. When your child wants to shoot an animal, let them inform you. Do not force it. When parents start pressuring their children to get the shot, it becomes something that the parent wants rather than what is best for the child. It should be acceptable if the youngster merely wants to follow the parent without participating. The effectiveness of a hunt can be evaluated in a variety of ways. The kill shouldn't be the only focus.

- ## Keeping Children in Harsh Conditions for an Extended Period

Adversity sometimes plays an important role in the adventure. However, if you're hunting in extremely cold weather, keep the hunt brief and make sure everyone is dressed appropriately.

It is generally recognized that keeping children in harsh conditions while hunting can have significant negative impacts on their physical, emotional, and psychological well-being. Here are some potential impacts:

Physical harm: Children who are kept in harsh conditions while hunting may be exposed to extreme weather conditions, dangerous animals, and hazardous terrain. This can increase the risk of injury or illness, which may have long-term health consequences.

Emotional and psychological harm: Being exposed to harsh conditions, such as extreme cold or heat, can be emotionally distressing for children. They may also experience fear, anxiety, or trauma from being in situations where their safety is at risk.

Disrupted education: Children who are kept in harsh conditions while hunting may miss out on regular schooling, which can impact their education and future opportunities.

Social isolation: Children who are kept in harsh conditions while hunting may have limited social interaction with other children and adults, which can impact their social development and ability to form healthy relationships.

Ethical considerations: Children may not have the physical or emotional maturity to fully understand the consequences of their actions or the ethical considerations surrounding hunting and killing animals.

• Unintentionally Creating a Failing Situation

Be sure your child has practiced using the bow or pistol they intend to use if they decide to try shooting an animal. Don't just hand your kid a gun on the day of the hunt and expect them to hit the target. Hurting an animal can ruin the thrill of hunting more. Every hunter encounters that occasionally, but a child can suffer severe consequences. Make every effort to stop that from happening. The likelihood of success increases if your child feels secure using the pistol or bow.

• Giving Your Children Your All

Let your children actively engage in the hunt's preparation and the day's events. Allow your youngster to prepare snacks, pack a backpack, use a map or compass to find their way, and choose a hunting location. If one of us shoots a deer, I prefer to let my kids see the blood trail, and I look for the chances to allow my kids to learn new things. Some of these tasks could be challenging, but let them try. We all gain knowledge from our struggles.

• Shaming a Child for Feeling Sorry Following a Kill

After a kill, children may experience sadness and even cry. When this occurs, some adults may discount or ignore their child's emotions or even unintentionally humiliate them for being depressed. It is advised to parents to validate their children's feelings rather than ignoring or shaming them. Take advantage of the chance to explain your youngster how hunting benefits the environment, produces wholesome meat for the table and offers a chance to enjoy nature.

- **Driven Too Hard to Go Hunting**

It's acceptable that not every child will want to go hunting. Avoid pushing it. Kids will be less motivated to achieve something if they feel more pressure. That's just how kids are. As you step back, your youngster might finally ask to leave. Don't be concerned if your youngster enjoyed hunting but stopped as a teenager. It's likely that after they reach adulthood, they will resume their hunting activities.

1.7 Hunting Morals and Manners

Be ready to incorporate these teachings into your child's hunting experience because no one else but you will teach them hunting ethics and etiquettes. Here are some fundamentals you ought to go through.

- o   Obtain permission before hunting on private property.
- o   Never presume that you may ask people to go hunting with you just because you have permission to do so on private property.
- o   Be considerate of all property and the environment.
- o   Retain the forest's original condition.
- o   Be considerate to other hunters and keep your noise to a minimum.
- o   Never point a gun toward anything other than a target or an animal you plan to shoot.
- o   Never fire a gun toward a house, a car, or a person.
- o   Give other hunters plenty of room when you are around.
- o   Support game management initiatives, sustainable wildlife organizations, and conservation efforts.
- o   Observe all rules and laws relating to hunting.

1.8 If You Aren't a Hunter?

If you don't hunt and your kid is interested in the activity, you probably don't know where to start. Consider your choices before telling them that there is no possibility of hunting out of panic. Do you have any hunters in your family? Friends? Coworkers? Don't be afraid to inquire because most hunters adore taking kids hunting. If they don't, they could know someone who does, who goes hunting and wouldn't mind a fellow student. Also, there are mentorship programs nationwide that match kids with adults who instruct and guide young hunters. Hunting clubs and sportsman's groups manage some, while others could be affiliated with scout troops. To learn more about your alternatives, start by getting in touch with nearby shooting and hunting clubs.

CHAPTER 2

SURVIVAL SKILLS: THE BASICS

Will your child survive if they get lost in the wilderness? Would they be able to protect themselves until aid arrive?

By taking these questions together, determine if your kid has wilderness survival abilities!

Our kids will find the world much less terrifying if they learn fundamental survival skills! Since children are always under the supervision of elders and are never left alone in the forest, many parents or educators may be perplexed as to why their kids must learn these skills. Even if your kids never need them, teaching them the basics of survival will boost their self-confidence and help them become more capable individuals who will succeed in life regardless of obstacles.

2.1 What Does the Term "Survival Skills" Mean?

Survival skills are methods one can employ to remain alive in any natural or artificial setting. In short, survival skills mean that people need to know how to survive in crisis. They are designed to offer the fundamental requirements for maintaining human existence, such as water, food, shelter, and other necessities. Children who acquire survival skills also learn moral principles and how to protect their safety. We must impart these abilities to our children and prepare them for any circumstance.

Along with instilling moral and ethical principles in our children, we must also think about teaching them fundamental survival skills. Many parents want the best for their kids and are constantly looking for ways to shield them from the harm of any kind. It's crucial to teach children about survival skills, so they only sometimes rely on us, even though we rigorously prepare ourselves and handle every conceivable disaster ourselves.

Risk assessment is the most fundamental yet crucial survival skill for young children. It is something we frequently take for granted as being "common sense."

The most extensive misunderstanding that most people have is this one. Consider how "common sense" might look to children if they had not been taught and exercised this skill before. As educators, give kids more chances to participate in risk assessment activities. For instance, while on a stroll in the park with your kids, ask them to point out any potential risks and hazards and discuss any necessary mitigation measures with you. Also, you could reassure them that there is no right or wrong response in such situations and what counts are their justifications.

2.2 Why Is It Crucial to Master Survival Skills?

Many of you might think that it is a worthless activity in today's society. Hunting, collecting, building homes, avoiding wild creatures, and avoiding dangerous settings no longer feel like necessities because we have progressed to such a degree as humans. After all, there is very little danger of our kids being lost in the woods or us losing our kids in a crowd in a strange city.

Children must be aware of all situations and have relevant, practical knowledge for everyone, whether or not they will encounter them in real life. Although we fervently hope and pray that none of our children will ever suffer injury, we must provide them with the necessary tools in an emergency. Even something as uncomplicated as a family camping or hiking trip might become tense if the child wanders off from the campsite or during the excursion. The research has found that 41% of grownups become lost in the woods even after leaving a trail and cannot find their way back, while kids who are naturally curious and fascinated by nature are even more vulnerable.

Hence, ensuring that our kids can and will survive whatever challenges they encounter is crucial. Even basic training can help them become more alert and receive assistance when required. Whether camping, hiking, or confronting a natural disaster, ensuring everyone in your family, especially your young children, has the skills they need for successful survival is crucial. In other words, you can start training your young children as early as five years old. What we mean by this is age-appropriate training skills that will help them in circumstances if and when necessary.

CHAPTER 3

SURVIVAL SKILLS: TOOLKIT

The importance of wilderness survival skills can be attributed to numerous factors. They can aid in your kid's survival if they find themselves in a precarious circumstance, which is one explanation. For instance, they can shield themselves from different dangers if they know how to construct a shelter. They can survive until help arrives if they know where to obtain food and water. Learning wilderness survival techniques is essential because

they can increase their enjoyment of the great outdoors. Your kids won't have to put themselves in danger to explore the environment if they can camp and walk securely. Knowing how to look after one outdoors will also help them enjoy nature's beauty more.

You should teach the following survival skills as soon as feasible to your kids. You can teach them how to survive in the woods by receiving basic cardiopulmonary and first aid training. You can help them prevent the typical issue of getting lost by having great navigational abilities. You can help them escape being gravely hurt or murdered when they have a safe hiding location during an unplanned night out. Teaching them how to treat and recycle untreated water can lessen the possibility of negative impacts. A navigational map, a compass, a GPS unit, and a smartphone app should all be kept in hand. Generally speaking, a knife, a multi-tool, and duct tape will suffice. They should be able to arrange safe and purified drinking water. A lightweight rain poncho or a tarp can create a windproof and water-resistant shelter. If they are running late for their check-in, they must provide contact information for the park rangers or the neighborhood first responders.

It doesn't have to be tedious to learn these abilities. Kids can learn and perfect survival skills by participating in games and role-playing scenarios. Always watch them for safety reasons, especially while working with intricate items.

3.1 Bush-Craft Techniques: How to Start a Fire?

The best way to learn skills like these is through practice rather than theory, so the next time you plan a camping or hiking trip, make it a point to use it as an opportunity to teach your kids about survival skills. Even something as simple as hiking through the woods or climbing a mountain can be turned into a teaching opportunity because you can share your observation by pointing out different geographical features and landmarks that will help kids find themselves if they get lost, which could be a lifesaving skill in a survival situation.

When you can camp in your backyard, there's no need to travel very far. It will allow kids to learn how to make a campfire and experience living without the conveniences they are accustomed to. Teach children how to gather firewood responsibly, including what kinds of trees and sizes of wood to look for, the value of selecting seasoned firewood, how to build fires safely, how to start flames in various age-fitting ways, and how to extinguish them afterward. Depending on age, you might want to teach your child how to make and use a fire to call for help.

Children should be taught to prepare and start a fire without a lighter or match. Although it may seem like a challenging undertaking, scores of stranded individuals succeed in doing so each day. In addition to keeping people warm, fire allows them to cook food, ward off wild animals, boil water to purify it, and keep insects and flies at bay.

Let's Set the Fire Kids!

Hey Kids! I'd be happy to help you learn how to safely and easily light a fire while camping!

Protection First

Gathering the covering tools before starting a fire is a wise idea. Keep a bucket of water nearby and a shovel for dousing the fire in the dirt. It is advisable to emphasize how crucial keeping someone near the fire is. Only let your fire burn unattended if it is entirely out and the coals are chilled to the contact.

The majority of beaches and camping areas have permitted fire rings. Choose a level location with little surrounding foliage if there isn't a fire ring and fires are permitted. But remember to glance up as well! Moreover, you must ensure no tree branches hang over your fire ring. The fire will be placed on a flat rock surrounded by a ring of rocks. Keep your fire small to safeguard the surrounding vegetation if there aren't specified fire rings.

Create A Fire Ring

First, you need to gather some supplies. You need dry wood, kindling (small sticks or twigs), and some form of fire starter. Some good fire starters include paper, dryer lint, cotton balls, or commercial fire starters.

Next, you need to find a safe place to build your fire. Look for a spot that's away from any trees or other flammable objects, and clear away any leaves, brush, or debris from the area. You can also build a fire pit using rocks or a metal fire ring.

Now it's time to start building your fire. Begin by lying down some small sticks or twigs in a teepee shape, leaving a small opening in the center. Then, place your fire starter in the center of the teepee. Light the fire starter using a lighter or matchstick.

As the fire starter begins to burn, blow gently on the flames to help them spread to the kindling. Once the fire is burning well, add some larger sticks or logs to the fire. Keep adding wood as needed to keep the fire going.

Remember to never leave your fire unattended, and always make sure it's fully extinguished before leaving it. To put out your fire, pour water over it and stir the ashes until they're cool to the touch.

With these tips, you'll be able to safely and easily light a fire while camping! Just remember to always be cautious and follow all fire safety guidelines.

3.2 Observing Your Environment

It's one of the most crucial skills to master for survival in any outdoor disaster even though it's not explicitly related to living in the wilderness or a natural setting. By beginning to identify landmarks and set up meeting locations for any emergencies, you may start teaching them this daily. When you take them for a stroll to school, go to the park while you're in the mall, go hiking, etc. In addition to educating them, you may help them put what they've learned into practice by occasionally testing them by having them walk through your home from a certain point. Moreover, you must teach your kids to cultivate the instinct or attitude necessary to remain composed and rational under pressure. Being calm can benefit them greatly because panic can lead people to make bad decisions. Use any outdoor family activities as a pleasant method to put the knowledge you have taught them to the test. It will allow you to determine how well they understand their surroundings and their situation awareness abilities.

3.3 Obtaining Water

Reap the benefits of the rain by sending children outside to gather rainwater using plastic containers, grocery bags, and baggies as a game. Whoever gathers the most is the winner. Further, show them how to suspend, spread, and partially bury the containers and other water collection techniques. Show children how to use a bandana or their shirt to filter rainwater.

3.4 Purification of Water

Since it's not sure if they would be able to obtain clean water, there are various methods of purifying water, such as boiling, distilling, and using water filtration tablets. It's advisable to bring water filtration tabs while camping to ensure safe drinking water. Additionally, teaching them how to locate water sources, identify unsafe water, and use primary filters like the Life Straw is essential for their safety and survival skills in the outdoors. Remember, prevention is always better than cure.

3.5 Easy Shelter Construction

Simple shelter construction is among the most crucial skills a youngster can learn. Every child should know how to erect a straightforward tent out of cordage and a sheet. Another excellent suggestion is teaching your child how to create a natural shelter out of supplies they find. It is a talent your family can master together for the rest of your lives. Construct a different kind of shelter each time you go camping or outdoors. You can even rehearse in your backyard. Children who comprehend the fundamentals of knotting can construct a shelter on tree trunks out of ropes and tarps. If not, youngsters can use it as a fort by building simple leaf houses and lean-tos, which are also simple to construct. Don't forget to mark the shelter to make it visible, to avoid frightening the animals and to draw notice from rescuers in an emergency.

Building a shelter while hunting can be a fun and educational activity for children.

Hey kids! Let me tell you how to build a simple shelter:

Choose a location: Select a spot that is dry and flat, and ideally protected from wind and rain. Look for natural features such as a large rock or tree that can provide additional shelter.

Collect materials: Gather materials such as fallen branches, sticks, leaves, and grass to use in building the shelter. Look for dry and sturdy materials that are easy to work with.

Construct the frame: Using the larger branches or sticks, create a frame for the shelter by leaning them against a natural feature, such as a tree or rock. Be sure to make the frame wide enough to accommodate the size of the shelter.

Create the walls: Once the frame is in place, begin to fill in the sides with smaller branches or sticks, weaving them in between the larger branches to create a solid wall. Children can also use leaves or grass to cover any gaps or holes.

Add a roof: Cover the top of the shelter with additional sticks or branches, laying them across the frame in a sloping pattern to allow rain or snow to run off. Cover the roof with leaves or grass to provide additional protection.

Finishing touches: Finally, add any finishing touches such as extra insulation or a layer of leaves or grass on the inside for additional comfort.

3.6 Tying Knots

Never undervalue the strength of a good knot! Given its numerous potential applications for saving lives, knot-tying is regarded as one of the essential survival skills in the wild, for instance, when constructing shelters, finding food, making tools and traps, etc. Also, it is a fundamental talent that helps to create the groundwork for the development of many other crucial skills. Children's fine and gross motor abilities, such as eye-hand coordination and asymmetrical bilateral integration, are improved by a simple knot-tying practice. Youngsters can begin this at home by engaging in basic tasks like tying shoelaces and ribbons, bundling long hair with rubber bands, or taking part in any rope adventure. Kids can start learning how to tie knots at a very young age. Teach your child various knots also how and when to use them for fishing, traps, snares, building shelters, etc.

3.7 Using A Compass, Map, And GPS

Kids should be taught how to comprehend a map and use a compass and GPS in case they become lost. It can be useful to help them return home. Children should be aware of their city and street address. Point out local features and landmarks close to your home, such as the petrol pumps, a water tower, library and rail tracks, etc. Coming back home from the grocery store, soccer practice, or school may become a game for young kids. Transform the process of learning navigation into an enjoyable experience by organizing a treasure hunt, where kids can create a map to help navigate and discover the prize while exploring the outdoors or visiting a park. Additionally, you can print city maps and highlight various bug-out routes to prepare for emergency situations while educating children on navigation skills. This fun and interactive approach can make navigation skills more engaging and help children develop crucial survival skills.

Teach map reading: Start by introducing the child to the different parts of a map, such as the legend, scale, and compass rose. Show them how to read the contour lines to understand the terrain and how to locate landmarks such as lakes, rivers, and mountains.

Practice map skills: Practice reading maps with the child by setting up a scavenger hunt or orienteering course. Encourage the child to use the map to find their way to different locations, and help them develop their map-reading skills.

Introduce the compass: Teach the child how to use a compass to orient the map and how to read the different directions. Practice with the child by having them navigate to different locations using the compass.

Use GPS: Introduce the child to GPS and how it can be used to navigate in the wilderness. Show them how to mark a waypoint and navigate it using the GPS device.

Emergency planning: Discuss what to do if the child becomes lost or separated from the group. Teach them to stay put and use the map, compass, or GPS to navigate back to camp or the meeting point.

Reinforce safety rules: Always emphasize the importance of staying safe while hunting, including staying together as a group, notifying others of their location, and following hunting regulations and guidelines.

3.8 Foraging

Foraging refers to the activity of searching and gathering wild edible plants, berries, nuts, and other natural foods in their environment. Foraging is an ancient practice that has been used by humans for thousands of years to obtain food and medicine from the natural world. Engage children in a fun and educational activity by introducing them to foraging. This experience will provide them with valuable knowledge about the natural world and stimulate their curiosity to explore their surroundings. Foraging can be an enjoyable and enriching experience that fosters a deeper connection with nature while teaching them about identifying edible plants, understanding seasonal changes, and appreciating the environment around them.

Explain to children which plants are harmful and which are edible. Take your kids on nature hikes while you identify the different flora and trees you come across. It will be useful on hikes and camping vacations. Some plants have dangerous lookalikes, and make sure kids verify their finds with you before consuming anything new.

Foraging for kids can be done in a variety of settings, such as parks, forests, meadows, and even urban environments. It is important to teach children to forage responsibly and to only harvest plants that are safe and legal to eat.

Some safety tips for foraging with kids include:

o   Always supervise children while foraging.
o   Teach children to identify plants correctly and to only pick those that are safe to eat.
o   Avoid foraging in areas that may be contaminated with pesticides, pollution, or other harmful substances.
o   Teach children to respect the environment and to only take what they need, leaving enough for wildlife and future foragers.
o   Always wash and thoroughly inspect any plants before eating them.

3.9 S.O.S. Making A Help Signal

Teach your kids basic signs or indicators for help if they become separated or disoriented while hiking in the woods. They should wear vibrant clothing so that they are noticeable from a distance. Discuss the usage of international distress signals if rescuers use land, air, or marine search methods. Pack them a whistle or a signal mirror and show them how to use it. In case of an emergency, campers can use a mirror to signal for help by aiming its reflection towards the camp's general direction. Additionally, blowing a signal whistle three times, waiting for a minute and blowing once more can help attract the attention of rescuers. This method is a practical and effective way of signaling for help when they are in distress while camping or hiking.

Here's how you can teach it to them:

- Start by explaining to your child what S.O.S. means. S.O.S. is a universal distress signal that means "Save Our Souls" or "Save Our Ship". It's used to signal for help when someone is in danger or in need of assistance.
- Demonstrate the signal to your child. The S.O.S. signal is made up of three short dots, three long dashes, and three short dots. You can use your arm to demonstrate the signal by holding it out straight and making the dots and dashes with your hand.
- Practice the signal with your child. Have them repeat the signal back to you and practice making it together. You can also make a game out of it by having them practice the signal while blindfolded or in a noisy environment to simulate an emergency situation.
- Discuss when to use the signal. Explain to your child that the S.O.S. signal should only be used in an emergency situation when they need immediate help. Examples of when to use the signal could include getting lost in the wilderness, being trapped or injured, or being in a dangerous situation.
- Make sure your child knows how to get help. In addition to teaching the S.O.S. signal, make sure your child knows how to get help in an emergency. Teach them how to use a phone to call 911 or how to find an adult to ask for assistance.

3.10 Overcoming Fear of the Darkness

Do they fear the dark? Get the kids off the settees and send them on a self-guided outdoor expedition. It is required in case of a bug-out that they must leave throughout the night. Start by going for evening strolls with them. Let children play flashlight tag with other kids instead. At night, turn off the electricity or the lights in the house and let your children exercise finding a flashlight and arriving at a predetermined meeting place.

3.11 Planned Evacuations

Have a plan with your kids for how you'll leave the house if something goes wrong. Discuss and put into practice safety measures for potential local emergencies such as tornadoes, power outages, hurricanes, wildfires, and floods. If your home is no longer a secure place to return to, choose a meet-up location and a backup. Also, drill the acronym S.T.O.P. into their minds.

S.T.O.P. stands for:

S - Stop
T - Take a deep breath
O - Observe your surroundings
P - Proceed with caution

Here's what each part of the acronym means:

Stop: This means that when you're in a situation where you're feeling overwhelmed, scared, or unsure, the first thing you should do is to stop. This gives you a chance to pause and take a step back from the situation.

Take a deep breath: Once you've stopped, take a deep breath. This helps you calm down and get centered. It's important to breathe slowly and deeply, taking in as much air as you can and then exhaling slowly.

Observe your surroundings: After you've taken a deep breath, take a moment to observe your surroundings. Look around you and see what's going on. Are there any potential dangers? Is there someone who can help you? What resources do you have available?

Proceed with caution: Finally, once you've assessed the situation, proceed with caution. This means that you should take your time and be careful as you move forward. It's important to be aware of any potential dangers and to take steps to protect you.

3.12 Outdoor Cooking Tips

Outdoor cooking is the next step after starting a fire. Most young children begin by learning how to make hot dogs. Also, understanding how to prepare and clean animals are crucial. Use this chance to educate children about penknives, knives and matters related to food safety, such as cooking temperatures and storage of food. Making "hobo bags" first is a fantastic way to get children interested in the subject. To accomplish this, you roast your meat and vegetables while they are covered in tin foil. A constant reminder is fire safety. You can then progress to more advance outdoor cooking techniques once they have mastered those.

3.13 Basic First-Aid

Create a variety of scenarios with their friends and allow them to take turns playing the patient and the person giving first aid to liven up their first aid training. Start by learning basic skills like how to bandage and clean a cut, make a sling, or make a transport sled out of a tarp and some limbs. Teach them how to assemble and use them to become familiar with the contents and applications of first aid kits. Discuss safety, prevention, and the best times to act in an emergency. It is crucial to start teaching young children about first aid and how to administer it right away. Children should be taught to utilize every item in the first-aid kit, what each one is used for, and how to use it. Therefore, show them how to utilize simple tools like bandages, cotton swabs, rubber gloves, safety pins, hand sanitizer, gauze, and other little, secure personal objects.

3.14 Self-Defense

Although they are only children, they should know how to fight and protect themselves. Every child should learn how to defend itself against a personal attack. Consequently, kids won't feel so powerless in stressful circumstances. Teach them or allow them to acquire some fundamental self-defense techniques. This skill will come in handy in various situations even when they have grown through puberty. Teaching self-defense techniques to kids can help them feel more confident and prepared in case of an emergency. Here are some basic self-defense techniques you can teach your child:

The palm strike: This is a simple but effective self-defense technique that involves using the heel of the hand to strike an attacker's nose or chin. Have your child practice striking a target like a punching bag or pillow to get comfortable with the motion.

The elbow strike: Another effective self-defense move is the elbow strike. This involves striking an attacker with the point of the elbow. Have your child practice elbow strikes on a padded surface to avoid injury.

The knee strike: If an attacker is close, your child can use a knee strike to strike their abdomen or groin. Have them practice raising their knee up and striking with the top of their knee.

The escape: Teach your child how to escape from a hold or grab. This can involve techniques like pulling away, twisting out of the hold, or striking the attacker to create distance.

The verbal defense: In addition to physical techniques, it's important to teach your child how to use their voice to defend itself. Teach them to be assertive and use a loud, clear voice to say "Stop" or "Back off" if they feel threatened.

Remember, the most important aspect of self-defense for kids is prevention. Teach your child to be aware of their surroundings, avoid dangerous situations, and seek help from a trusted adult if they feel threatened or unsafe.

3.15 Weather Trends

You may teach your children to observe weather trends at any age so they can at least get some early signs of adverse weather. As kids get older, it will be beneficial to teach them how to pay attention to the weather, how to check weather forecasts, and what to do in the adverse weather. Children should be taught the warning signs of severe weather, including cyclones, hurricanes, thunderstorms, sand storms and the safest places to seek refuge during each disaster. Simply noticing slight variations in the weather can give your kids ample time to seek shelter before it's too late in a survival crisis.

Teaching kids about weather warning signs is important to help them stay safe and prepared in case of severe weather conditions. Here are some steps you can follow to teach kids about weather warning signs:

Start with the basics: Begin by teaching your child about different types of weather conditions, such as thunderstorms, tornadoes, hurricanes, and blizzards. Explain what causes these weather events and the potential risks associated with them.

Use visual aids: Using pictures, videos, or diagrams can help your child visualize the different types of weather conditions and their warning signs. You can also use weather apps or websites to show them real-time weather updates and warnings.

Talk about warning signs: Once your child is familiar with different types of weather conditions, teach them about the warning signs that indicate severe weather is approaching. For example, for a thunderstorm, warning signs can include dark clouds, lightning, thunder, and strong winds.

Practice identifying warning signs: Take your child outside and ask them to point out any warning signs they see. Encourage them to observe the sky, the wind, and other environmental cues to identify potential weather changes.

CHAPTER 4

HUNTING ESSENTIALS

Before sending children into the woods, make sure they have the bare necessities: pants, sweatshirts, jackets, face masks, hats, belts, gloves, layers, eye paint, a youth hunting rifle (if you feel confident using one), or minor self-defense tools like a knife.

4.1 How to Recognize Animal Tracks?

Learning to recognize various animal tracks is another survival skill that children can pick up quite early. When they are small, this could be a game to keep them entertained and having fun. You can encourage children to find and follow game trails or other traces as practice for hunting or trapping as they get older and can explore on their own. Teach them how water flows downhill, how to detect streams or pools of water, how to check for animal footprints that may point to water sources and other things when you explore the outdoors or hike together.

4.2 How to Use a Pocket Knife?

Trust your child and give them a pocketknife when old enough. Kids can use it for various tasks, including fruit peeling, bottle opening, fishing, whittling wood for arrows, and even self-defense. Do not forget that it's still a weapon; instruct them to handle it carefully. Be sure you and your child are aware of abiding by the rules in your community governing the carrying of pocketknives.

4.3 Encountering Wildlife

Children of all ages are naturally curious about any wildlife creatures they may encounter. Some children may react to animals with an innate fear or panic, which increases the danger by provoking an animal to strike or flee away and getting hurt when they trip, fall, or run into a tree or another dangerous place. Teach your children how to react if they come across a harmful animal.

Teaching children how to react when they come across a harmful animal in the forest is important for their safety. Here are some steps you can follow to help children learn to react appropriately:

Identify potential harmful animals: Begin by teaching children about the types of animals that they might come across in the forest that could pose a threat to their safety. For example, snakes, bears, or wildcats.

Teach them to stay calm: Instruct children to remain calm if they see an animal that they perceive as harmful. Explain that most animals will not attack unless they feel threatened, so it's important to avoid doing anything that might provoke them.

Explain how to react: Depending on the animal, teach children how to react appropriately. For example, if they come across a snake, they should stand still and back away slowly. If they come across a bear, they should speak in a calm voice, avoid direct eye contact, and slowly back away.

Role-play different scenarios: Practice different scenarios with children, so they know how to react appropriately in each situation. Role-play different animal encounters and ask children to demonstrate how they would react.

Remind them to seek help: Explain to children that if they feel threatened by an animal, they should seek help from an adult or a park ranger as soon as possible. Tell them to avoid running or screaming, as this can provoke the animal.

4.4 Hiding for Protection

A game of hide and seek can be helpful in facing an emergency. Kids will become more accustomed to the many hiding places in your house as they play this game. Instruct them to remain hidden in case of emergency until you or another responsible adult approaches. Remind them that they should leave the house and meet you at the agreed-upon location in case of a fire rather than hiding. Children are adept at discovering hiding places, so the next time you're out in the woods; you might play a game with your kids to see who can locate the best shelter fastest. Just keep an eye on them so they don't wander off and get lost.

4.5 If Lost, What to Do?

A parent's worst fear is losing their child in a crowded place. Instruct the kids to stay at the same point in case you lose contact with each other because it will be more challenging to find them if you both start looking for each other. A water bottle, whistle, neon bandana, cell phone (you may call an emergency without network) or walkie-talkie, and other survival gear should be packed in their backpack for signaling and keeping hydrated until you can locate them. Children should be taught the value of maintaining body heat and the need to consider refuge if they become lost in a natural setting. One of your main goals should be to teach them how to build or find shelter because if they get lost, they might become exhausted, cold, and hungry, which would make it difficult for them to find shelter before nightfall. You can accomplish this by demonstrating them how to build modest buildings, find temporary shelter in hollow trees or caverns, etc.

CHAPTER 5

FISHING ESSENTIALS

Fishing can be a great activity for kids while hunting, as it can help them learn about nature, practice patience and concentration, and enjoy the outdoors. Here are some fishing essentials for kids to have while hunting:

- **Fishing rod and reel:** A basic fishing rod and reel is essential for any fishing trip. For kids, it's important to choose a rod and reel that are easy to use and comfortable for their size.
- **Tackle box:** A tackle box is a container for storing fishing gear such as hooks, lures, sinkers, and line. Kids can decorate their tackle box with stickers or paint to make it their own.
- **Bait:** Depending on the type of fish you're trying to catch; you'll need different types of bait. Worms, minnows, and crickets are popular choices for freshwater fishing.
- **Fishing line:** A strong, durable fishing line is important for reeling in a fish. Monofilament line is a good choice for beginners.

- **Bobbers:** Bobbers are small, floating devices that attach to the fishing line and help you see when a fish is biting.
- **Pliers:** Pliers are handy for removing hooks from a fish's mouth.
- **Sunscreen and bug spray:** Protecting your skin from the sun and insects is important when spending time outdoors.
- **Snacks and water:** Fishing can be a long and tiring activity, so it's important to bring snacks and water to stay hydrated and energized.
- **Fishing license:** Depending on where you live, you may need a fishing license to fish. Be sure to check the regulations in your area before heading out.

By having these fishing essentials, kids can have a fun and successful fishing experience while hunting. They can learn about the different types of fish, how to cast a line, and how to be patient and persistent while waiting for a bite. When imparting survival skills to children, the significance of food safety should not be disregarded. Children must be aware of the appropriate cooking and storage temperatures for food and how to hunt food like fish. If your children have allergies with some food, teach them how to inspect their food for ingredients they are allergic to and what to do if they eat something with those ingredients.

5.1 Safe Swimming

Swimming is a survival skill that everyone should acquire. Enroll kids in swimming lessons in your neighborhood, or if you live near a small lake or river, teach them yourself. Put a focus on water safety, particularly how to accurately judge water depth and current. Educate your kids about avoiding accidents and water safety. Among the topics to think about are:

- Never dive or jump into the water without first checking its depth and the presence of any submerged rocks, pipes, sharp objects, etc.
- Ensure your kids understand that they should shout for aid; toss a life preserver or other flotation device, run for help, etc., when a friend or another person is in trouble in the water instead of diving in to try to save them from drowning. Kids need to understand that someone who is drowning will panic and drag him or her down with them.
- Teach your children how to measure ice thickness and spot signs that the ice is thinning or melting.
- Assist your children in learning about currents; tides, and other aspects of how water functions so they can make wise judgments if they encounter difficulties in the water. When they need to cross water, especially in a bug-out situation, you never know when they might require.

5.2 Where and How to Fish?

Children can start learning where to catch fish from a very young age. Ensure kids understand where to get bait, what kind to be used, and safe fishing techniques. Show children how to recognize fish, when the best times are to go fishing, and how to use a pole, a net, their hands, or even a t-shirt if necessary. Let them practice as much as possible to master techniques like unsnagging a line, removing a hook from a fish, and self-baiting a hook.

Fishing can be a fun and educational activity for kids, but it is important to teach them safe fishing techniques to ensure their safety and the safety of others. Here are some tips on safe fishing techniques for kids:

Wear a life jacket: Make sure that all children wear a properly fitting life jacket while fishing. Even if they know how to swim, a life jacket can provide extra safety and protection.

Use barbless hooks: Barbless hooks are easier to remove from a fish's mouth and can reduce the risk of injury to both the fish and the child.

Handle fish with care: Teach children how to handle fish gently and avoid touching their gills or eyes. Use wet hands or a wet cloth to hold the fish and support their weight properly.

Respect the environment: Teach children to respect the environment and to follow fishing regulations and guidelines. Encourage them to properly dispose of any trash and to avoid fishing in areas that are protected or designated as "no fishing" zones.

Practice casting safety: Teach children to be aware of their surroundings and to avoid casting near other people or objects. Encourage them to cast away from themselves and to use caution when casting in windy conditions.

Be prepared for emergencies: Have a first aid kit in hand and teach children what to do in case of an emergency, such as a hook injury or a fishhook in the skin.

5.3 Cleaning and Preparing Fish

Teaching your children how to clean and cook each fish is a wonderful idea if you train them to catch the fish.

In a SHTF or survival situation, catching, cleaning, and cooking fish can go a long way towards keeping them nourished.

SHTF is a term used to refer to a situation where an unexpected disaster or crisis occurs, such as a natural disaster, economic collapse, or civil unrest, that disrupts normal life and requires individuals to be self-sufficient and prepared to survive without external support. Teaching the term SHTF to kids can be a difficult task, but it is important to educate them on the importance of being prepared for unexpected events. Here are some tips on how to teach the term SHTF to kids:

Explain the concept in simple terms: Use age-appropriate language to explain what SHTF means, emphasizing the importance of being prepared for unexpected events and the need to be self-sufficient.

Explain the concept in simple terms: Use age-appropriate language to explain what SHTF means, emphasizing the importance of being prepared for unexpected events and the need to be self-sufficient.

Focus on safety and preparedness: Explain that the goal of being prepared is to keep oneself and one's family safe in case of an emergency. Teach kids about basic emergency supplies, such as food, water, first aid, and how to develop an emergency plan.

Use real-life examples: Use real-life examples of natural disasters or other unexpected events to help kids understand the concept of SHTF. This can include stories from the news or personal experiences.

Practice emergency drills: Practice emergency drills with kids, such as fire drills or earthquake drills, to help them understand what to do in case of an emergency.

Encourage independence: Teach kids the importance of being self-sufficient and self-reliant in case of an emergency. Encourage them to learn basic survival skills, such as starting a fire or building a shelter.

CHAPTER 6

SMALL GAME HUNTING

Small game hunting teaches skills, including dog handling, safe rifle handling, and accurate shooting.

When they first start hunting, young kids would frequently go after quail, rabbits, and squirrels in the fields and woodlots close to their homes. Small games make up a sizable portion of the weekly supper menu for many families.

6.1 How to Hunt Small Game?

Learning to track and hunt small wild game and fowl is one of the life skills that youngsters can acquire at a young age. Start by classifying any animal footprints you come across in your yard or on the farm. If they are old enough, young children can join adult-supervised hunting excursions using an age-appropriate firearm, a slingshot, or another alternative weapon. Even young toddlers can learn how to catch small wildlife (rabbit, squirrel) using snares and other traps.

Small game hunting can be a fun and educational activity for kids that help them develop skills such as patience, observation, and outdoor awareness. Here are some tips to help kids get started with small game hunting:

Choose the right gear: Kids should have appropriate hunting gear, such as a properly fitting camo jacket and pants, sturdy boots, and a hat or cap. They should also have a hunting license and follow all state regulations.

Practice shooting skills: Kids should practice shooting skills with a responsible adult prior to hunting. They can use air rifles or low-powered 22 rifles to practice shooting at targets and get comfortable with the equipment.

Learn about the target species: It's important for kids to learn about the small game they will be hunting, including their habits, habitats, and behaviors. They can use field guides or online resources to research the species they will be targeting.

Choose the right location: Kids should hunt in areas where they are likely to find small game, such as wooded areas, fields, or along water sources. They should also have permission from the landowner before hunting on private property.

Hunt in a group: Kids should always hunt with a responsible adult or in a group of peers who are also experienced hunters. This helps ensure safety and provides opportunities for learning and guidance.

Use ethical hunting practices: Kids should follow ethical hunting practices, such as making sure they have a clear shot before firing, minimizing the suffering of the animal, and using all parts of the animal they harvest.

Small game hunting can be a rewarding and educational activity for kids. It helps them develop valuable skills and an appreciation for the natural world. It's important for kids to follow safety guidelines and ethical hunting practices, and to seek guidance from an experienced adult when learning how to hunt.

6.2 Cleaning and Preparing Small Game

Kids must be taught how to properly clean and prepare the small game animals they hunt, just like they do with fish. Most adults lack small game cleaning and butchering skills, but youngsters can acquire them if they are capable and motivated enough. If your children know how to properly slaughter and clean animals, they could be valuable group members in a survival situation if you aren't there.

Cleaning and preparing small game is an important skill for kids to learn while hunting, as it allows them to make use of the animals they catch and appreciate the importance of sustainable hunting practices. Here are some steps kids can take to learn how to clean and prepare small game:

Learn about the anatomy of the animal: Before cleaning and preparing the animal, it's important for kids to understand its anatomy. They can use a field guide or online resources to learn about the different parts of the animal and how they contribute to its overall structure.

Choose the right tools: Kids will need some basic tools to clean and prepare small game, such as a sharp knife, a cutting board, and a container for the meat. It's important to choose tools that are appropriate for the size of the animal and easy for kids to use safely.

Start with simple game: Kids should begin with simple game like rabbits or squirrels, which are easier to handle and require less preparation than larger animals.

Follow proper safety precautions: Before handling the animal, kids should wash their hands and wear gloves if possible to prevent the spread of disease. They should also be careful when using sharp tools and keep them away from their body and other people.

Skin and gut the animal: To prepare the animal for cooking, kids will need to skin and gut it. They can start by making a small incision near the anus and carefully cutting through the skin and muscle to remove the intestines. They can then use a knife to skin the animal and remove any unwanted parts, such as the head and feet.

Clean the meat: Once the animal is skinned and gutted, kids should rinse the meat thoroughly with cold water and remove any remaining hair or debris. They can then cut the meat into smaller pieces for cooking or storage.

By learning how to clean and prepare small game, kids can gain a deeper appreciation for the animals they hunt and the importance of sustainable hunting practices. They can also learn valuable skills that can be applied in the kitchen and in other areas of life. It's important for kids to follow proper safety precautions and to seek guidance from an experienced adult when learning how to clean and prepare small game.

Activity Pack for Kids

Your kid must be excited about their next hunting expedition. Here is a pack of interesting activities that your kid can do on his hunting trip.

Have a break.... Match The Following

Hunting

1. An antler of at least 3 inches long on a deer.
2. Firearms such as pistols, revolvers, and rifles.
3. The use of dogs for recreational wildlife tracking.
4. A device, such as a rod or narrow board, used for launching darts.
5. An individual who leases and resides on at least 5 acres of land.
6. Optical instruments that use light-amplifying circuits powered by electricity or batteries.
7. The act of offering something for sale or exchange for compensation in any tangible form.
8. The act of attempting to locate, pursue, or search for wildlife.
9. A hand-held device.
10. To provide consent for an action to be taken.

A. pursue
B. night vision equipment
C. bow
D. antlered deer
E. permit
F. firearms
G. atlatl
H. lessee
I. sell
J. chase

Let's Hunt the Words

```
G Q L W T U F N O I T A V R E S N O C I
X I S R M N S D Q E U Y O K H Q L T U X
N I E O A D V E P M T E A U D B S G H N
L E O P O C M J R A O B H R X F J A G F
S L X O F R W T L Y R U I N S G U B K C
P N W Z E K V F M J K B W K L E A V E S
S L T E U O A A I Y P O C I S V T G H R
V K D P P L E O X Z U I Q M N O O C A R
S S C R L H W T Y R T Q O L K Y M F S B
Y Q C A E D B C V S W Z Y O Q P G E D K
V J U A R L N J I B S B S U I N D H D T
L M R I M T T A B I N O Q C I A M A B M
T I Y G R O E N T I F I M T O R Y T Y L
S O L P Y R U R A S Z N O U Q V D F H
E S S A R A E F U X E U U T W E U J G J
K K S E B J P L L T H E O I C V G Q W C
F Y C Z F D A E M A A T R J P C Z U X O
O H U A C O R N Q Z G N U T B V T V X M
U N M T K A D B W J K E T O G G M Y M M
W Y M V Z W P S D G U E F P W F F H T Q
```

1. LEAVES
2. ACORN
3. MOSSY OAK
4. DEER WORD BANK
5. TREESTAND
6. BUGS
7. ANTLER
8. SQUIRREL

9. TRACKS
10. BIRD
11. BOAR
12. STICKS
13. TREES
14. NATURE
15. FALL
16. HUNTING

17. CONSERVATION
18. CAMOUFLAGE
19. WOODS

64

Nature Scavenger Hunt

1. Name a type of insect.
2. Identify a type of tree that bears flowers.
3. Describe a cloud that has a distinct shape.
4. Choose a smooth stone from a river.
5. Point out a nest built by a bird.
6. Identify an animal that is making a sound.
7. Name a type of tree that keeps its leaves all year.
8. Choose a type of seed pod from a plant.
9. Describe a type of fungus that grows on trees.
10. Find a stick that resembles a particular letter of the alphabet.
11. Identify a type of fuzzy caterpillar.
12. Look for footprints left by an animal.
13. Find a branch that has a knothole in it.
14. Choose two different types of leaves from different plants.
15. Look for an object that can be rolled.
16. Identify an empty snail shell.
17. Find a rock with a hole in it.
18. Identify a structure built by bees.
19. Find a rock that can be used for writing.
20. Identify an animal that goes into a deep sleep during the winter months.

Camping

Find the given words.

```
K P Y U R L A R E I T C R P D B H S B C L X N
S A R V Z C I Z W Q U X V K B I G N I M W R K
H N S I G I F X N C C B L X Y F G V L T P Z X
X N S A D L A Y O V J A X Y H C E A H D O X A
I E M X H V X F R K N G F I J E R N S M L S S
G I I Y Z C I C U T N P R Y S R T R H Y O C L
T D N P E J G E L K L L O W Q I E U M K I E T
E L W C F H L B D X N I U G I M H T R J G V H
N W M G Y U E H F C L S E K W A T E B J W T L
I L G W S I N A N J P N D E K P E A M S N T G
T F I F E S R O T J T G I L L K B L G B S I F
R I W Y Y N C E A O E E S A A Z S W L R M I I
G P S O N V T L S X N E T B N X I O P T I A H
E E U H N P I Y Y N T H O Q G T H N S N M I K
A H G C Q F N N I A O D T G M N A C P G I P X
A K E O G C F T A A N S T I Y F P M N C C T H
```

1. MNACPGI
2. INGIBK
3. AHBEC
4. AEGRT
5. AXIGLENR
6. SMINWMG
7. HNSIGIF
8. MIMSNWGI OLOP
9. ITSNAATFC
10. XIGTENI
11. SCEVTTIIAI
12. EWNORULDF
13. RLAREIT
14. TENT
15. NCEAO
16. FCERIMAP
17. FESROT
18. HIFGLHTLSA
19. KELA
20. OUEDIST
21. NRUTEA
22. EEGNSILP GAB
23. IWKLANG
24. EIDLWLFI
25. TEH !TEBS

66

Forest Maze

Help the hunter find his way out of the forest

Camping

Find the given words.

```
C F H A F Y W J U S H S U R B R I A H Q A R E E
B J E M U U L I M D O O W G V W Q S H D P N P V
B T H S U N R F C Z Q S W A G T O Z L S V X K N
C I I W V D X Q W H S U K A D H D C Q A D S I N
E M K S A R Y T I P E R I F H S H D D I M U I Q
H G I E L I D S S A R G I D I R T U H C G I X U
X R N V H V O Y A H E R S H E Y K I S S I N N B
H A G A F M D Z X K P T N O I X W H Y F N O P A
J S B E S G Q O U M F O R N R U V H G C J K Z W
C S O L E X T B L T T H O W G H B U L H V Z Y B
E H O G M F Z V U I S Q V S J U X W F Y E U M U
P O T H K O F I C P T D S E M A G D R A O B K T
I P S J G Z U S G Q I U S B V M X R L E S J S T
B P V A O R S L R X C A P G B Y A J I A X T N E
O E Z U N O B O L F K S P W A S L A B Y G S W R
O R Z D M R S E A D S I Q Y E B D W Z Z C W C F
K M U X A K Z T V L I L X I G M G Z U X F D O L
S O M R T F P S L Y K Q R R P L K N D L V C X I
A C Z U L N Q N G K O T J L L I M U I Q C D D E
L J J A Q N R P T O E R V L L Y L A D P L F U S
M U M N P C J H P L G A D E Q E K Q L T G E A S U
T E K S T E K C I R C A S C B A H W O Q V E D G
S S D F J H N O H Q F X R F B S H S D W P V L Y
O V R L K C T G Z D W A T E R B O T T L E Y H S
```

1. HERSHEY KISS
2. LEAVES
3. FLY
4. SLEEPING BAGS
5. BOOKS
6. ANIMALS
7. TOILETRIES
8. FLAMES
9. MAT
10. SEADS
11. BUTTERFLIES
12. CRICKETS
13. GRASS
14. BOARD GAMES
15. HIKING BOOTS
16. WATER BOTTLE
17. GRASSHOPPER
18. PILLOW
19. WOOD
20. FIRE PIT
21. DIRT
22. HAIR BRUSH
23. STICK

Word Search

```
F R J K P I E E A A W S X Q P R N H E
C O H D L A N E C L K I H A O S P N K
B T E R O H S X E M T H N N W L O S I
M O Z K R T H L F N O K E J N C T A P
E M C U O K T R B E K E V D G S E K B
I X A L E R Z H Z M W R Z G U E E O Z
P P L Y G W R E T Y F F A S L S L O L
N B O B B E R E R S C A S T E N H H O
G Z W U I S L N S U C Y I L O E E C H
P W M O B O Z I R H L A K Y S C A T B
V O K E R M R T X D C C T P A I D U H
L N R I F M M Y G H A E M F R L X J E
P N M P P Y K T J T T A E V I A B I R
U I W P Z M L N D A A S W L T S C E V
K M U A J S Q X O D A E B R O J H K X
J U M R Z H R B G I K R O V G S M A P
W P K C V N F W N C N L L I G E U L B
F T E K C A J E F I L Q B X C W E W E
T J R E T I B S W I V E L P Y F V A J
```

1. LEECH
2. POND
3. LICENSE
4. RELAX
5. LIFE JACKET
6. SHORE
7. LINE
8. SINKER
9. BASS
10. BITE
11. BLUEGILL

12. BOAT
13. BOBBER
14. CARP
15. CAST
16. CATFISH
17. CRAPPIE
18. HOOK
19. ICE
20. LAKE
21. LET'S GO FISHING
22. LURE

23. STEELHEAD
24. MAP
25. SWIVEL
26. MINNOW
27. TACKLE
28. MOTOR
29. TROLL
30. PIKE
31. WORM

Hunting

1. HWIET LAIT _____

2. URSETS _____

3. NERBOTWI _____

4. BOW ADN OAWRR _____

5. ETEVELV _____

6. KONC _____

7. AELBT _____

8. UNTINHG _____

9. ERET NTSDA _____

10. ESCTN _____

11. NASLTER _____

12. IDAEYRTMX _____

13. HIFGCETNL _____

14. RVIUQE _____

15. ZZLMEU ELDOAR _____

16. BDIADEOSR _____

17. NCMOPDUO _____

18. ELMCUFGOAA _____

19. ILFED RDSNISGE _____

20. CAESRP _____

Solve the crossword puzzle.

Across

4. S
8. A
12. catfish catcher
13. H
15. Hatch
18. You hunt for ones
19. U
20. Twinkle twinkle
7. Y
25. B
9. Y

31. Has long tall antlers
10. Hunters buddy
32. Short stubby tail
11. T
47. Buck or doe
48. K Down
1. H
2. G
3. Night sight
5. Color of money
6. Fast car
26. camander

27. Mice chasers
28. A
29. J
30. Honker
43. Netflix
46. Heart burn
33. M
14. G
35. A biding website
16. H
37. K
17. N

40. C
42. L
44. H
45. Chevrolet
21. Summer hangout
22. Computer messages
23. Can't see me
24. H

Reading Comprehension Time

Rice grains were scattered by the hunter on the net. He concealed himself behind the bushes and awaited the arrival of the birds. A group of young pigeons, along with their leader, were flying in that direction. They spotted the rice grains on the ground and exclaimed with delight.

"Yum, yum!" they exclaimed. "Let's go down and feast!"

They decided to have a party and enjoy the rice grains.

Answer the questions given below.

Q. Where did the hunter spread something?

A. _____

Q. Where did the hunter conceal himself?

A. _____

Q. Which birds noticed the rice grains?

A. _____

Q. What was the reason for the pigeons' descending?

A. _____

CONCLUSION

We are running out of excuses not to regularly engage in outdoor activities. The benefits are limitless and with proper guidance, we can teach our youth to make the most out of their trips. After carefully going through this guide, you can be much better prepared for an outdoors adventure in the woods with family and friends. These activities will help you teach your young ones to be more responsible, self-sufficient and confident for their next hunting expedition. Most importantly, it will boost their self-belief and promote a positive outlook towards everything else in life. Again, parental guidance is mandatory.

Teaching children how to travel through nature is a crucial ability that might have various advantages. The advantages of learning to travel around the great outdoors are diverse and extensive, whether it's to foster a love of nature, increase confidence and independence, or improve problem-solving abilities.

There are several potential threats, including animal attacks, storms, injuries, and insect stings. Even a hike that initially looked safe could quickly become fatal. All of this is not being offered to scare you or make you stay indoors. We never really think about getting into trouble in the woods with our kids, and maybe they never will. But even as we encourage our kids to enjoy being outside, we also need to provide them with the knowledge and abilities needed to deal with any situations that might happen.

Made in the USA
Columbia, SC
25 June 2025